Contemporary chinese
interiors

CONTEMPORARY CHINESE INTERIORS
Copyright © 2005 PAGE ONE PUBLISHING PRIVATE LIMITED

FIRST PUBLISHED IN 2005 BY:
Page One Publishing Private Limited
20 Kaki Bukit View
Kaki Bukit Techpark II
Singapore 415956
Tel: (65) 6742-2088
Fax: (65) 6744-2088
enquiries@pageonegroup.com
www.pageonegroup.com

DISTRIBUTED BY:
Page One Publishing Private Limited
20 Kaki Bukit View
Kaki Bukit Techpark II
Singapore 415956
Tel: (65) 6742-2088
Fax: (65) 6744-2088

Editorial/Creative Director: Kelley Cheng
Editor: Bernard Chan
Assistant Editor: Ethel Ong
Editorial Co-ordinator: Ethel Ong
Key Designer: Huang Yulin
Format Designer: Tan Lijuan
Layout & Illustrations: Huang Yulin
Assisting Team: Meng XinXin & Shaun De Souza

ISBN 981-245-196-X

Colour Separation by SC Graphic Technology Pte Ltd
Printed and bound in China

Contemporary Chinese
interiors

Bernard Chan Chun-leuk

PAGE ONE

Contents

introduction 006

eu yan sang 008

t8 014

dragon-i 020

zenses 026

lotus passion 032

grand shanghai 038

hu cui 046

baishayuan teahouse 056

club by the lake 064

xintiandi yi hao lou 068

yong jin lou 074

glimmering silkworm 082

090   dong lai shun restaurant

098   crystal jade kitchen, singapore

104   yi jia xian

110   shanghai mian

116   heaven and earth

122   crystal jade restaurant, shanghai

128   marunouchi cafe

134   peerless teahouse

142   jin jin hall

148   suzhou cha ren cottage

154   cheena restaurant

160   haikou new world garden resort clubhouse

166   ye shanghai

172   michel house

182   si chuan dou hua restaurant

190   designer index

192   acknowledgements

introduction

China is fast becoming an economic power and with that comes fast development and changes in the people's lifestyles, living standards and contemporary culture. This rapid development in a country with rich history and culture has brought about a unique evolution in Chinese design trends and styles. Traditions provide a strong background to new designs, bringing about a harmonisation of the old and the new, with the exploration of contemporary design concepts. Such contemporary Chinese designs that showcase a unique palette of textures, colours and elements is representative of Chinese roots and at the same time present a set of aesthetics that is appealing to the modern world.

In recent years, contemporary Chinese designs have not only become popular in Asia, they have also gained a strong following in the western world. It is the intention of this book to bring together a selection of projects from the Asian region including China, Hong Kong and Singapore showing various fine examples of this fusion of East and West approaches. The result of this juxtaposition creates a new dimension blending both culture in harmony and balance. Hopefully this will inspire designers the world over to continue to bring this design phenomenon to a higher level.

Turn the page and indulge yourself in a world where acid jazz plays against traditional Chinese lanterns and antique furniture.

008

Located in Hong Kong's Telford Garden Plaza, *Eu Yan Sang* sits within a section of the shopping arcade dedicated to Chinese herb and health supplement stores.

When *Eu Yan Sang* decided to branch out from their two existing retail shops in Hong Kong, they brought in Joseph Sy & Associates to design the latest in the series. The result – instant success. The design of the outlet and new product packaging, part of a bid to create a new image for the company, has already made a strong impact in consumer market awareness. The total rebranding, from design and packaging to advertising and positioning, encapsulates *Eu Yan Sang* with a modern contemporary look that reflects its East-meets-West philosophy. It is a delicate balance between tradition and science, the old and the new. The move has also made *Eu Yan Sang* approachable, moving them closer to the modern retail environment.

photography Joseph Sy   **designer** Joseph Sy   **design firm** Joseph Sy & Associates   **location** Telford Garden Plaza, Hong Kong

(opposite page) View of the museum area from within the shop

(this page: top left) View of the back of the shop where two mirrors visually extend the width of the shop

(this page: top right) The horizontality of the shop, accentuated by linear shelving, strips of wood flooring and running ceiling light recesses

(this page: bottom) Illuminated acrylic boxes displaying a variety of herbs

(this page: top) View of the shop entrance from the exterior with the original *Eu Yan Sang* signage, written in Chinese characters

(this page: bottom) View from the entrance to the museum where a display panel describes the history of *Eu Yan Sang* and the practice of herbal medicines

(opposite page) A glass window with a graphic approach: Chinese characters and English words are used as part of the shop's facade design. The adjacent series of photographs explain the manufacturing process of *Eu Yan Sang's* products.

The original shop's design scheme was inspired by the medicine boxes commonly found in most traditional Chinese medicine stores. In this Telford Garden shop, the only thing retained from the past was the colour scheme. Designed to enhance the unit's width, the shop is crafted with a strong play of horizontality that is extended further with the use of a mirror at the end wall. Scattered gondolas previously used for product displays are now replaced by a simple terraced rack. Details of other cabinetries were simplified to allow products to stand out. A brilliant play of light adds and enhances both ambience and products.

Eu Yan Sang's shop front carries subtle Chinese characters on the display window denoting its name. A small section dedicated as a 'museum area' offers consumers brief knowledge of herbal products and the process of transforming them into medicine. It also educates consumers on how to distinguish genuine herbs from imitations, and how to classify top grade herbs from the low. The ambience of this section is kept subdued. A deep burgundy colour dominates the area, while lighting is provided only on the specimen displays and informative literature.

014

t8 restaurant and bar

Hidden away in one of the nineteenth-century Shikumen houses located in Shanghai's most unique dining and entertainment development, *T8* has acquired a reputation as Shanghai's finest international restaurant and bar rave from residents and visitors alike. It is listed in Conde Nast Traveler's 2002 "Hot Tables" as one of the top 50 "world's most exciting restaurants".

Situated in Shanghai's trendy Xintiandi area, *T8* offers a delightful culinary and sensory experience with its unique mix of savoury food and designer ambience. Featuring dramatic interior lighting and design from Japanese designer Yasuhiro Koichi, *T8* recreates a captivating yet relaxing Pan-Asian atmosphere accented with an inlaid modern fountain and paintings by Chinese artist Pang Yongjie. The approach of the design adopting east-west features truly reflects the fusion food it celebrates in this unique environment.

photography Gary Edwards **designer** Yasuhiro Koichi **design firm** Design Studio SPIN **location** Xintiandi, Shanghai

(opposite page) Intimate lounge dining

(this page: top left) The restaurant's show kitchen

(this page: top right) Bar seating along the restaurant's show kitchen

(this page: bottom left) The entrance hall

(this page: bottom right) A private dining area

At *T8*, patrons can opt for a seat at the wrap-around bar to view the chef and his team at work in the glassed-in show kitchen or select a more discrete place by the carved wooden screens. The modern cuisine prepared by *T8*'s team of international chefs features variations on both western and Asian menus, exemplifying the team's culinary creativity and years of experience at world-renowned restaurants.

The ambience is dark, somber, with a generous serving of sophistication. The establishment's design, like its menu, is a perfect fusion of modern design aesthetics and traditional building materials. Classic timber lattice screens defining pockets of intimate dining areas are set against dark wood furniture with sweeping modern lines, as full-height glass windows are composed with raw stone floors. The lavish play of materials, added to details like custom-made bamboo door handles and traditional-looking wall lamps, make up the many intricacies that make *T8* a vision of class.

(this page: left) A glass cabinet at the back of the bar

(this page: top right) Bar chair and table lamp

(this page: bottom right) Counter seats at the bar

(opposite page) The restaurant's show kitchen and counter dining area

dragon-i

Dragon-i **may be** better known for its celebrity spotting with a gamut of international guests that runs from movie stars to socialites and even soccer players, but above the nightly myriad of activities, it is ultimately the masterfully carved interior that makes it a class above the rest.

The whereabouts of the bar/lounge/restaurant was thoughtfully determined – masterminds behind *Dragon-i* opted for a less-frequented locale in hope of whittling out a niche clientele of its own, while positioning it just a stone's throw from the popular hangout Lan Kwai Fong. With the building constructed against a slope, access to the establishment can be either through an escalator from below, or via an open-air stairway from above.

photography Kelley Cheng **designer** India Mahdavi, Hervé Bourgeois and Guillaume **design firm** IMH Interiors and gbrh **location** The Centrium, Central, Hong Kong

(this page) Circular red booths with plush cushion seats add to the dynamism of the restaurant section

(opposite page: top) Red phoenix-print lanterns of varying sizes bathe the space in a warm, sensual glow

(opposite page: bottom) The intense red hues of the main dining section

The site sets the scene for a different entertaining experience. There is no conspicuous entrance or frontage to the bar - a welcoming terrace quaintly performs the job. The terrace, which serves the dual functions of a reception and outdoor bar, takes up almost half of the 3,000 square footage and is decked out with beige leather armchairs and birdcages. There stands what just might be the largest birdcage that one would ever see - measuring in at a diameter of three metres, it spans the full height of the space. Made from thin strips of bamboo stems, the huge birdcage is integrated with birdcall recordings, creating a tranquil air that stands in stark contrast with the groovy tunes blasting out from the adjacent dance floor.

Large panes of glazing draw a casual separation between indoor and outdoor spaces. Beyond the line, timber flooring gives way to a seamless, textural surface. The space within is divided into the Playground - a dance and bar area, and the Red Room - the main dining section, demarcated by timber relief screens. Red and circular elements abound, adding to the dynamism of the irregular form, and echoing the colossal structural column imposed on the interior setting. Red phoenix-print lanterns of varying sizes bathe the space in a warm, cosy hue of light, while the round booth seating occasionally printed with dragon motifs prompts intimate conversation.

Another much talked-about feature of the nightclub is the unisex bathrooms. Clad in shimmering silver mosaic tiles, all seven bathrooms come complete with their own toilet, sink, mirror, paper holder and dustbin, all fashioned in a unifying metallic finish that matches the envelope.

It is hardly a coincidence then that even the managers' outfits were sponsored by Jean-Paul Gautier. Be it the interiors, furniture, lightings, food or even the people, the quest for perfection in *Dragon-i* is relentless.

(opposite page: top left) The huge birdcage spans the full height of the terrace

(opposite page: top right) The discreet and welcoming entrance terrace

(opposite page: bottom left) Round booth seats prompt intimate conversation

(opposite page: bottom right) The terrace, decked out with beige leather armchairs and birdcages

(this page: left) The terrace

(this page: right) Looking up at the terrace ceiling

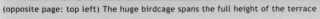

zenses

(this page) The massive wood slate doors of the main entrance

(opposite page) View of the bar through a screen of sculpted branches partitioning the dining hall

Located in a modern office building within the hustle and bustle of Hong Kong's financial district, *Zenses* restaurant and lounge provides a tranquil haven with fusion cuisine set amongst a unique atmosphere. Off the building's ground floor main entrance, two elevated massive wooden slate doors act as canopies, marking the entrance to the establishment. Situated next to the entrance, a take-away counter set against an illuminated 'light box' wall draws the attention of the passersby.

photography Chester Ong   **designer** Ed Ng and Dan Lee   **design firm** AB Concept Limited   **location** Henley Building, Hong Kong

(opposite page: top) View of the peripheral dining booths, tucked into an angled wall niche and embraced by raw, variegated timber boards

(opposite page: bottom left) The massive wooden slate entrance doors transform into canopies when raised

(opposite page: bottom right) View of a private dining room, showing stained oak furniture adorned with classic lines

(this page) The imposing red pendant lamps are given a touch of drama by the angled mirror behind

(this page) View of the main dining area from the bar and lounge

(opposite page: top) The passageway leading from the lounge into the main dining area

(opposite page: bottom) A forest of sculpted branches and towering vertical screens heighten the restaurant's concept of layering

Zenses' extraordinary ceiling height is one of its most distinguishing interior features. Upon entering the main dining hall, the ceiling height increases dramatically and opens up into an impressive double volume space. During the day, natural light floods in from the front entrance, filling the restaurant with an earthly glow. The overall design of the restaurant is minimal, with subdued tones and dark stained oak furnishings. Pockets of colour punctuate the dark canvas of the restaurant with the use of bright red pendant lamps. The lamps, lit up like oversized Chinese lanterns, dangle seductively over the bar area while an adjacent angled mirror further emphasizes the theatrical effect. In this section, the floor is raised with fewer tables, functioning also as a lounge area.

Though the layout of *Zenses* is straightforward, its interior spaces are divided in an elaborate 'layering' approach. Using sculpted branches as a screen, the designer creates a soft partitioning of the dining hall. Vertical screens with oversized tropical foliage, placed in front of the peripheral dining booths, further enhance this sub-division of space. In fact no two walls are parallel in the dining hall. Exaggerated angles emphasise heights and depths in the interior, while the furniture takes backstage with simple shapes and classic straight lines in stained oak and vinyl covers.

(this page) Strikingly Contrasting colours of black and gold are used throughout the restaurant

(opposite page) A layering effect is achieved here with the use of different materials and various elements

lotus passion

Located in the tranquil podium of a high-class business building in the city center, *Lotus Passion* is a place where one can enjoy tea, snacks and meals.

Black and gold dominates the palette of the 650-square metres two-storey establishment. Every space is thoughtfully designed – the designers created various layouts of seating and partitions that lead to exquisite smaller compartments. The result is a series of unique spaces, each with their own character. The first floor features five cones that are skillfully placed among the bar and the seats, while the second floor displays more privacy and discreetness with the use of brown beaded curtains, lavender gauze drapes and crystal glassware, creating a sense of warmth and an overriding cosy ambience.

photography Courtesy of Talent Architecture **designer** Zheng Yao **design firm** Talent Architecture **location** Yangyu Xiang, Suzhou City

The logo of the teahouse, based on the pattern of a lotus, appears at random throughout the interior. A central void is designed with black lotus-shaped lattices running from top to bottom, forming a strong contrast of shadows and lighting effects when set off by the nearby gold-foil wall covering. Modernity and tradition, simplicity and rich ornaments are all fused together in this remarkable interior.

The theme of this establishment is to pursue the new and re-discover the old that when combined, creates an interior of harmonious coexistence.

(this page: left) A lounge area on the upper level

(this page: top right) Private seating areas enclosed by gold partitions become the focal points of the interior

(this page: bottom right) View from the entrance

(opposite page) Bright orange cushions and decorative crystal glass elements contrast the dark upholstery of the sofa

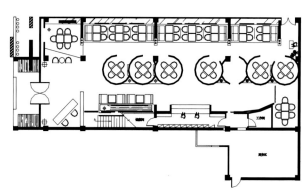

First storey floor plan

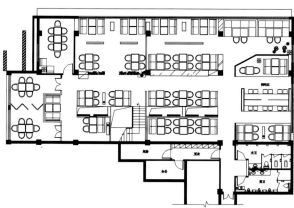

Second storey floor plan

(opposite page) The colour gold dominates the second level

(this page: left) Cosy armchair seating areas line a corridor, defined by a subtle raise in floor height

(this page: right) Glass vases are placed along the corridor as ornamental glass beads shimmer like golden raindrops

038

grand shanghai

Touted as Singapore's first authentic Shanghainese restaurant, *Grand Shanghai* is literally yesteryear Shanghai recreated and transplanted into a modern restaurant setting. Painted in a palette of olive green, red, yellow and mahogany, the atmosphere within the restaurant is intriguing and dramatic.

Occupying a generous 10,000 square feet, the restaurant houses a main dining hall and four private dining rooms that are each decorated in a different theme and era. Tucked along the side of the restaurant, a wine bar and a section of booth seating overlook the riverfront on one facade of the restaurant. The highlight of the restaurant is a proscenium stage that fronts the main dining hall, where live performances by musicians are put up nightly. The gesture, reminiscent of fine dining establishments back in the day, succeeds in giving *Grand Shanghai* its charming almost romantic charm. Giant fabric pendant lamps casting yellow light upon rows of circular tables and booth seating arranged around the hall seemingly transports one into the middle of a grand banquet in Old Shanghai.

photography Kelley Cheng   **design firm** EC Studio Manila Inc.   **location** Grand Copthorne Waterfront Hotel, Singapore

(opposite page) The wine bar section with booth seats, tucked along the side of the restaurant

(this page: top left) A section of booth seats overlooking the riverfront

(this page: right) Trompe l'oeil murals cover sections of the restaurant's walls

(this page: bottom left) View of the main dining section, set with crisp white linen tables, European wine glasses and Chinese tableware

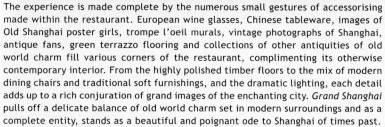

The experience is made complete by the numerous small gestures of accessorising made within the restaurant. European wine glasses, Chinese tableware, images of Old Shanghai poster girls, trompe l'oeil murals, vintage photographs of Shanghai, antique fans, green terrazzo flooring and collections of other antiquities of old world charm fill various corners of the restaurant, complimenting its otherwise contemporary interior. From the highly polished timber floors to the mix of modern dining chairs and traditional soft furnishings, and the dramatic lighting, each detail adds up to a rich conjuration of grand images of the enchanting city. *Grand Shanghai* pulls off a delicate balance of old world charm set in modern surroundings and as a complete entity, stands as a beautiful and poignant ode to Shanghai of times past.

(this page: left) The highlight of the restaurant: a proscenium stage that fronts the main dining hall, where live performances by musicians are put up nightly

(this page: top right) Giant fabric pendant lamps cast yellow light upon rows of circular tables and booth seating arranged around the main dining hall

(this page: bottom right) The restaurant's palette of olive green, red, yellow and mahogany sets the mood for an intriguing and dramatic atmosphere

(opposite page) Contemporary dining in old world settings; *Grand Shanghai* is a picture-perfect ode to yesteryear Shanghai

(opposite page) One of the individually designed private dining rooms

(this page: top left) The private dining rooms – hidden behind solid Mahogany doors adorned with decorative brass handles

(this page: right) The toilets of *Grand Shanghai* are designed to reflect the restaurant's old world charm

(this page: bottom left) Collections of antiquities fill the various corners of the restaurant, complimenting its otherwise contemporary interior and furnishings

(this page) "Sandwalls" form an interesting layer of wall texture within the restaurant, evoking feelings of naturalness and rusticity

(opposite page) The alluring entrance of *Hu Cui*, with a long dark flamed granite catwalk flanked by silk-screened glass and bottom-lit with soft diffused light

hu cui

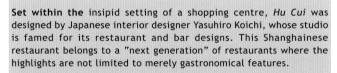

Set within the insipid setting of a shopping centre, *Hu Cui* was designed by Japanese interior designer Yasuhiro Koichi, whose studio is famed for its restaurant and bar designs. This Shanghainese restaurant belongs to a "next generation" of restaurants where the highlights are not limited to merely gastronomical features.

The entrance into *Hu Cui* is an elaborate expression of a long dark flamed granite catwalk flanked by silk-screened glass and bottom-lit with soft diffused light. As one moves along this passageway, the subtle forms, sounds and smells of the restaurant's activity surface sensuously from behind the silk-screened glass walls.

Entering the dining hall, elements such as timber screens carved in Chinese motifs and wall panelling set with Japanese fabrics lend an Oriental flavour to the otherwise contemporary dining arrangement. In a broad sweep, the design expresses the designer's understanding towards Shanghai as one of the greatest melting pots of China, blending Eastern traditions and Western cultures.

photography Kelley Cheng   **designer** Yasuhiro Koichi   **design firm** Design Studio SPIN   **location** Ngee Ann City, Singapore

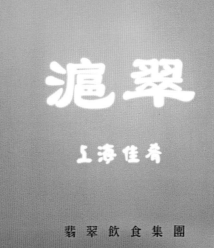

(this page: left) Timber screens carved in Chinese motifs and wall panelling set with Japanese fabrics lend an Oriental flavour to the otherwise contemporary interior

(this page: top right) A closer view of the Japanese fabric wall panelling

(this page: bottom right) The restaurant's main dining hall

(opposite page) Furniture carved with Oriental motifs reflect the Eastern theme of the restaurant

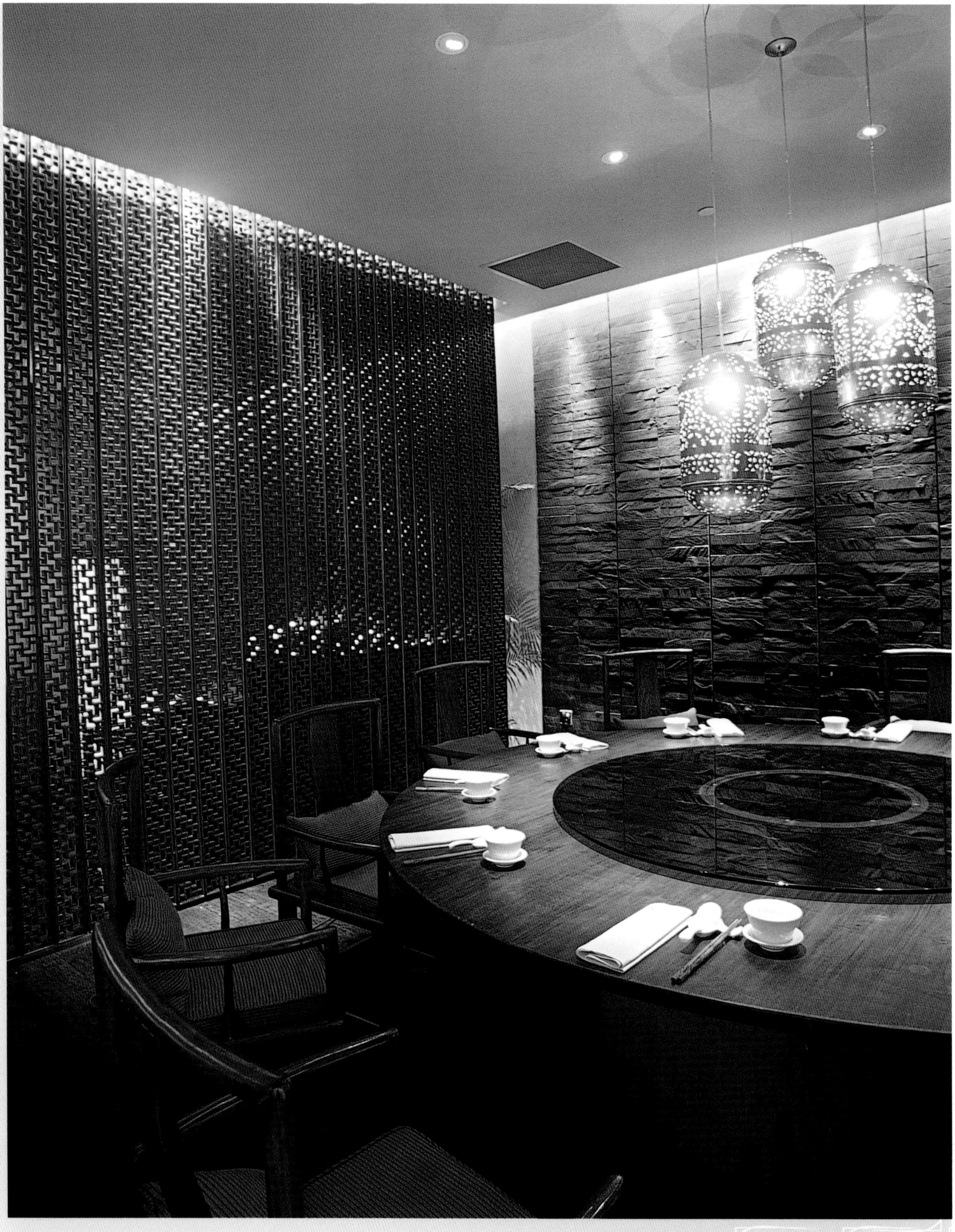

(opposite page) Western-style seating, poised against a mix of modern and old materials, hint at the fusion of various cultures within Shanghai

(this page: left) One of the private dining rooms within the restaurant

(this page: right) At the end of the entrance passageway, a hostess's podium stands ready to greet guests

Seeing every installation of furniture or decoration as an art piece, Koichi has imbued painstakingly within each and every piece a meaningful sense of reason for existence. In fact, the fabric wall panelling actually depicts the flow of the tides of time from past till present and into future. Illuminated in different angles and varied in orientation, the panelling form art pieces in themselves, representing the multiple facets of people, life, cultures and societies.

At the same time, timber screens carved in Chinese motifs, reminiscent of the Chinese ping feng and demarcating passages or spaces within the dining hall, inject a characteristically Eastern element into the restaurant. "Sandwalls" composed of compacted earth, colouring and bamboo fibre, form an interesting layer of texture in the treatment of walls within the restaurant. Undressed to its raw sensuous form and set alongside the fabric panelling and slate-clad walls, these sandwalls invoke in one a feeling of naturalness and rusticity.

In step with the client's longtime intention to set up a wine bar, the addition of *Lau Ling Bar* at the rear of the restaurant - enterable by the other entrance - formed the ideal solution to negotiate the differences between the two ends of the site. In the early stages of design, the existence of this additional entrance on the other end of the site, fronting the main street, was what prompted Koichi to consider further options on exploiting the full spatial capacity of the site.

In *Hu Cui*, the entire experiential concept of fine dining is explored and leads the pack in defining a whole new perspective in Chinese restaurant design. From the western-style banquet seating to the mix of modern and old materials and the fusion of various cultures, Koichi has left pockets of hints for the patron to discover upon incidence or chance, all without verbal or written rationalisation, and quite simply, just experience.

(opposite page) One of the private dining rooms with a long banquet table

(this page: left) "Sandwalls" within the interior, undressed to its raw sensuous form

(this page: right) Art plays a big part of the restaurant's design, with intricate art pieces gracing its various corners

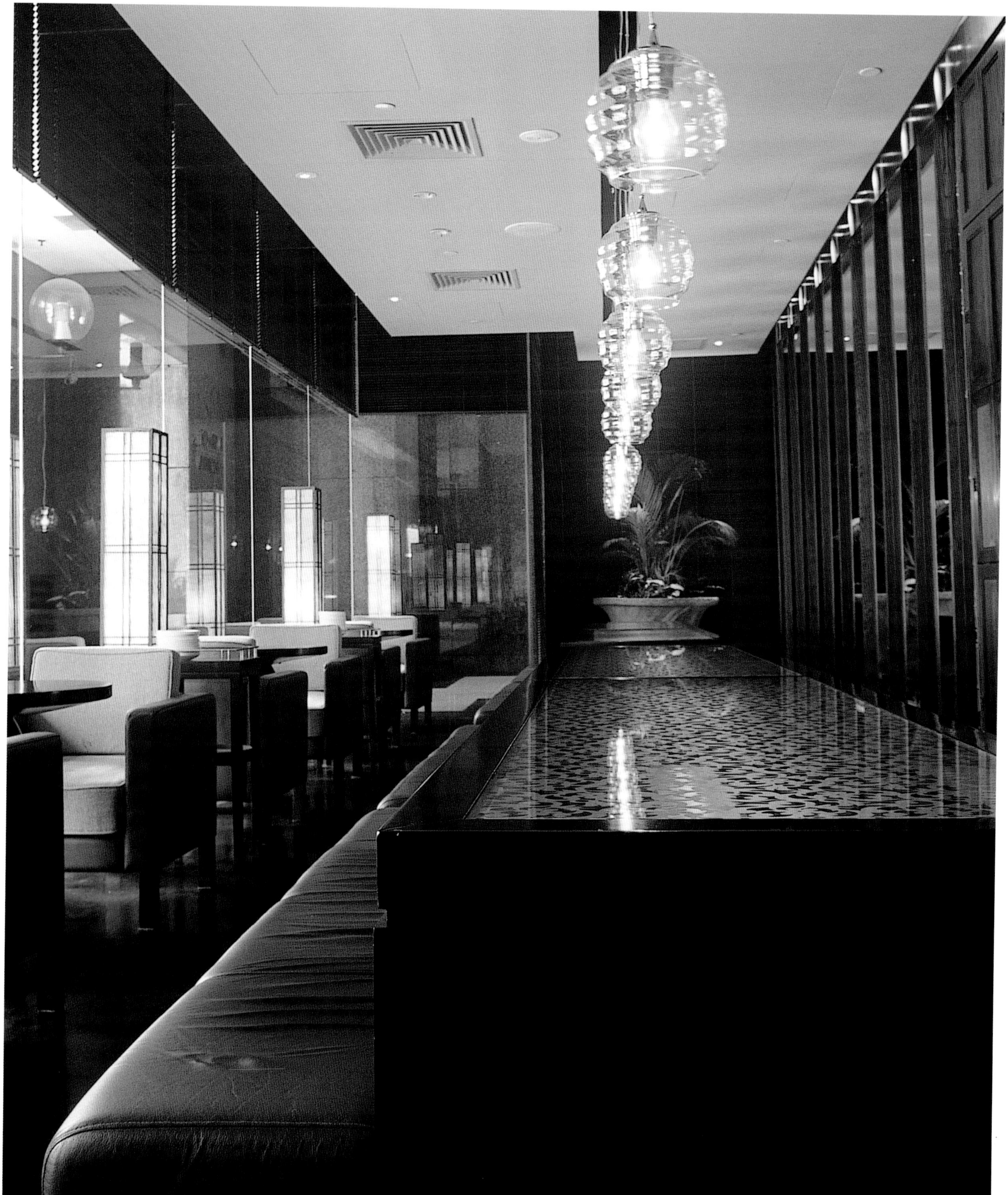

(opposite page) The dark and sensuous interior of *Lau Ling Bar*

(this page: left) Bar counter seats grace a section of *Lau Ling Bar*

(this page: right) Plush armchairs make for intimate conversations within *Lau Ling Bar*

baishayuan teahouse

Located in Changsha, the capital of Hunan province in China, this 3-year-old Chinese structure was fostered and adapted by the current owner to create a trendy, contemporary teahouse. While maintaining the Chinese character and spatial value, the building was carefully transformed.

Baishayuan Teahouse is situated right in front of the Baisha Park where there is a well-preserved "thousand-year-old well" on its side, supplying mineral water to the nearby inhabitants for many generations. From morning to dawn, throngs of people stream in and out to get the water from the well for drinking, tea making, bathing and various other uses. With its long history dating back to the Ming Dynasty, the people of Changsha have crowned this old well as the "Fountain of Life".

photography Alvin Chan **designer** William Lim and Alan Chan **design firm** Alan Chan Design Company **architect** CL3 Architects Limited **location** Baisha Park, Changsha, Hunan, China

(this page: top left) A retail section offering souvenirs like cultural books, teapots and tea

(this page: top right) Adjacent to the open gallery, a spacious room with benches and mosaic tables provides an alternative space for tea

(this page: bottom) An alcove with exquisite sofas creates a more intimate area for enjoying tea

(opposite page) The staircase floating above the fishpond is perceived as a separate element detached from the building. Vertical wooden fins further define the boundary

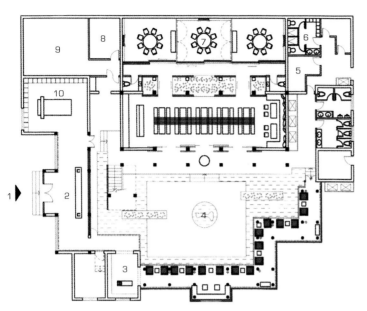

First storey floor plan

1 entrance	6 w.c
2 reception	7 v.i.p room
3 library	8 storeroom
4 pond	9 kitchen
5 office	10 souvenir shop

(this page: top) An interplay of geometry with the underside of the roof, wood partitions, and the row of pendant lamps

(this page: bottom left) The exterior courtyard of the two-storey building with a fishpond as the focal attraction

(this page: bottom right) A glass column displaying teapots punctuates the reception and hostess desk. The glass is fused together by a new technique of heat welding to give a clean and crisp look

(opposite page) The corridor of the upper level is surrounded by a transparent glass enclosure and uplighters illuminating the underside of the pitch roof

The architecture of *Baishayuan Teahouse* is based on the design of traditional Suzhou Gardens with the building outline preserved for keeping the cultural uniqueness of the local city. Inside the building, there is a thorough constructional change of the interior to achieve a new contemporary look for serving high-profile customers such as government officials, artists, designers, cultural workers as well as tea lovers.

The building is divided into three main areas: a retail section, an open gallery and the two-storey main building. The open gallery is enclosed with full-height clear and red glass, forming a contemporary tea lounge with an exquisite sofa sitting area. Wood screens are added for shading while chic furniture bring comfort to guests. Materials like cement screed, whitewash, slate, wood screens and glazing are employed throughout the interior, giving the place its modern yet traditional look. In the two-storey building, the upper floor was set-aside for VIP guests while the ground floor provides a contemporary seating environment looking into the garden where live performances take place during special Chinese festive seasons. Fishponds and bamboos are introduced as focal elements in the courtyard.

The use of various linear elements – screens and columns – at the *Baishayuan Teahouse* is in harmony with the existing traditional Chinese architecture, capturing the spirit of "east meets west" and reinterpreting it into a uniquely styled Chinese teahouse.

(opposite page) An informal lounge overlooks the open
courtyard

(this page) A glass wall encases an open deck surrounded
by lounge seating

Second storey floor plan

1   void
2   projection screen
3   void

club
by the
lake

The building is situated on Xingye Road between the culturally important First National Congress Hall of the Communist Party of China and the newly created Tiaping Qiao Park and Lake. Its sensitive location dictated that no signage or advertising was permitted and no obvious alterations to the original external fabric of the building were to be made. *Club by the Lake* was the second private club to take part in the Xintiandi development project in Shanghai.

The original building, like most of Xintiandi, is a Shikumen or 'Stone Gate' house. Built-in grey bricks with terracotta detailling, the house is an excellent example of the style prevalent in the 1920's when Shikumens were becoming more elaborate in style. Main entrance doors surmounted by a carved terracotta pediment open into a small courtyard, with a roof - introduced together with a new staircase - that grants access to the upper floor.

The ground floor is about 330 square metres and consists of a reception area in the original courtyard space, with bronze revolving doors that open up into a stone and brick lobby. A carp pool sits under the stairs, with water flowing from an antique wine jar. Original glazed and panelled screen doors open into a lounge and bar area that is designed for exhibitions and performances. An elaborate period fireplace in carved teak provides the accent feature to this room as original stained glass panels illuminate the bar. Furniture is a combination of original mother of pearl inlaid blackwood with contemporary velvet couches. Colourful silk lamps illuminate the seating area, providing seductive, low light to the space.

photography John Butlin   **designer** Stephen James   **design firm** Plan 3 Asia Limited   **location** Xintiandi, Shanghai

The upper floor consists of a bar, lounge area, main dining space, two private rooms and service areas. The main dining space has a six-metre high ceiling that exposes the building's original slate roof tiles and timber beams. An island bar features an original stained glass panel screen acting as a divider and bar back. Accent walls are lined in iridescent shot silk with the colours of the silk complementing the stained glass. The private rooms are lit by skylights, diffused sunlight streaming in through the glass prisms.

Throughout the interior, carpets are custom-made to reinterpretate art deco patterns in modern colours. The furniture here is similar to those on the lower level – a combination of antique blackwood and upholstered modern pieces, accented with silk pillows and runners.

The result is magical - intricate detailing, traditional colours pitched against modern furnishing, and low, seductive lighting – *Club by the Lake* is the perfect example of the strength and beauty that can emerge from interpreting traditional architectural elements through modern eyes.

068

This private clubhouse was opened in 2000 as a club and exhibition space for the developer Shui On, and for the use of high-ranking city officials. The original building was built in 1925 in red brick and stone detailing as a private residence. It is one of the most elaborate buildings in Xintiandi. The architectural style is typical of the period of the free-standing Shikomen style buildings.

The building's facade is almost entirely original and is a very elegant example of the period. Stone steps sweep up to original glazed entrance screen doors carved with calligraphic poems. On each level, fine plaster ceilings, elegant woodwork, original windows and doors were carefully restored during the reconstruction.

photography John Butlin   designer Stephen James   design firm Plan 3 Asia Limited   location Xintiandi, Shanghai

(this page: top) Ground floor exhibition and gallery space with original plaster ceilings

(this page: bottom) A private dining room on the top floor

(opposite page: top) An upper floor dining room with original windows opening onto a terrace

(opposite page: bottom left) The penthouse area for private gatherings

(opposite page: bottom right) The bridge at the ground floor entrance with a carp pool running alongside

(this page: top left) View towards the ground floor lift lobby

(this page: right) The three-storey sky-lit atrium with balconies and original timber structures

(this page: bottom left) The lounge bar adjacent to the atrium

(opposite page) The lounge bar is comfortably furnished with upholstered pieces, antique Xinjiang rugs and lit with aged green glass desk lamps

The building facade on Taicang Road has entrance doors leading into a triple volume atrium with balconies surrounding it. This space, originally open to the sky, has a carp pool and granite bridge lined in blue granite leading to the exhibition space and lift lobby. The second level houses an intimate bar and piano that opens on to the atrium. The room is comfortably furnished with upholstered pieces, antique Xinjiang rugs and lit with aged green glass desk lamps.

The building's interior was redesigned to provide larger, more practical spaces that were better suited to its new role. However, a great deal of effort was made during the reconstruction to maintain and restore the building's original features and grandeur. Fireplaces were reinstalled with original hearths and the staircase was strengthened and rebuilt. Original ironwork was repaired and repainted to the initial colour schemes.

Chinese period furnishings were sourced and placed throughout the club while original furniture pieces were located and duplicated. Many original antiques were incorporated along with paintings, lamps, ceramics and so on. Art deco carpets on each level were designed and manufactured using traditional hand-weaving techniques that required many months of production.

Under the roof eaves, a small private space was created for the owner to host smaller, more intimate gatherings. Simply furnished with antiques and modern pieces, the sloping timber clad ceilings create a cosy and relaxed space rarely seen by most visitors.

yongjin lou

During the Sung Dynasty, *Yong Jin Lou* was the setting for lavish celebratory banquets, thrown for the winners of the Imperial Examinations. Today, this restaurant is the setting for many celebration lunches and dinners.

As a clubhouse for the Xihutiandi Development in Hangzhou, *Yong Jin Lou* sits on the very same site as its Sung Dynasty predecessor. The 3-storey restaurant sits along a row of nondescript buildings in the Old People Park, on the banks of the West Lake; its only redeeming feature being the setting and its traditional tiled roof.

The restaurant was styled after the garden pavilions of the Sung and Ming periods – the high point of traditional Chinese gardens. Large windows open up on every level, maximising views of the West Lake and the surrounding gardens. The windows, framed in intricate timber screen work, capture magnificent views of the environment.

photography John Butlin   **designer** Stephen James   **design firm** Plan 3 Asia Limited   **location** Xihutiandi, Hangzhou

(this page) The carved screen doors of the ground floor

(this page: left) An adjacent window with intricately carved brickwork

(this page: right) A corridor flanked by glazed wooden screens

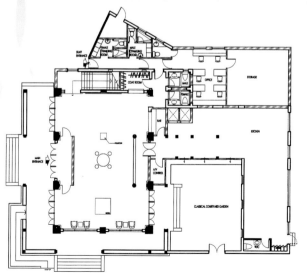

First storey floor plan

(opposite page: top) A view of the second floor dining area

(opposite page: bottom left) The waiting area on the second floor uses antique Rosewood and Blackwood pieces, upholstered in modern embossed velvets and Hangzhou silks

(opposite page: bottom right) The lounge and bar area on the top floor

(this page: bottom left) The lounge and bar area on the top floor

(this page: bottom right) The six-metre high roof structure and its exposed beams and original clay roof tiles, seen here from the top floor dining area

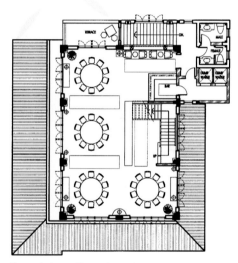

Second storey floor plan

(this page) Watching the sun set over West Lake from the restaurant's ground floor balcony

(opposite page: top) Looking at the new windows and screen work from the exterior

(opposite page: bottom) View of the ground floor dining area

An existing external staircase takes guests to the upper floors, while a courtyard garden was created between the main building and an adjacent single-storey building, used as a kitchen and service space.

Full-height windows in carved timber and glazed blue and white bevelled glass surround the ground floor reception area. The space, used for exhibitions and audio-visual presentations, allows glimpses of the lake, gardens and courtyard. The area is furnished in classical Blackwood furniture and antique blue and white carpets, and is a befitting prelude to the rest of the interior.

The staircase leading up to the other floors boast carved granite steps, and its walls traditional polished clay tiles. A moon window framed in intricately carved brickwork sits at the foot of the staircase, casting the space in an enigmatic light.

The second and third floors offer dining spaces and beautiful, framed views of the lake and gardens. The furnishings on these floors combine antique Rosewood and Blackwood pieces, upholstered in modern embossed velvets and Hangzhou silks. The third floor features an exposed six-metre high roof structure with exposed beams and clay roof tiles. At night, uplighters highlight the roof while candle-lit lanterns illuminate the space, creating a soft warm glow both inside and outside.

Externally the building relies on the carved timber window screens, white painted walls and old clay roof tiles to evoke an imagery of the past. Extensive landscaping of the entire park completes the setting of the building, offering guests a glimpse into a different time.

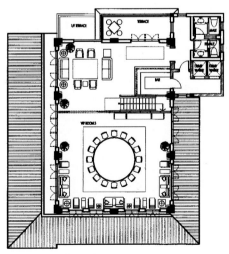

Third storey floor plan

glimmering silkworm

Located on one of the major commercial streets of the Huangzhou, the small two-storey restaurant offers afternoon tea and set dinners, offering a retreat where people can find peace and relaxation from the hectic world outside.

On the ground level is the entrance hall, bar, and seating areas while the second level is dedicated to more discreet with half-enclosed seating spaces. The whole design is based mainly on three key elements – steel, cement and glass, with the intention to communicate a sense of architectural articulation. In addition, colourful abstract artworks and an oversized cane artifact inject a mysterious Oriental flavor.

photography Courtesy of Talent Architecture   **designer** Zheng Yao   **design firm** Talent Architecture   **location** Wulin Road, Huangzhou

(this page: top) Colourful accent furnishings and fabrics compliment the traditional and natural materials within the interior

(this page: bottom left) The glass-covered entrance area leading into the restaurant

(this page: bottom right) Looking out to the entrance area and rattan sculpture from the first floor dining area

(opposite page: top) The original building patio was transformed into part of the second level dining area

(opposite page: bottom) The second floor dining area is enriched by sunlight, ever changing shadows and fresh furnishings

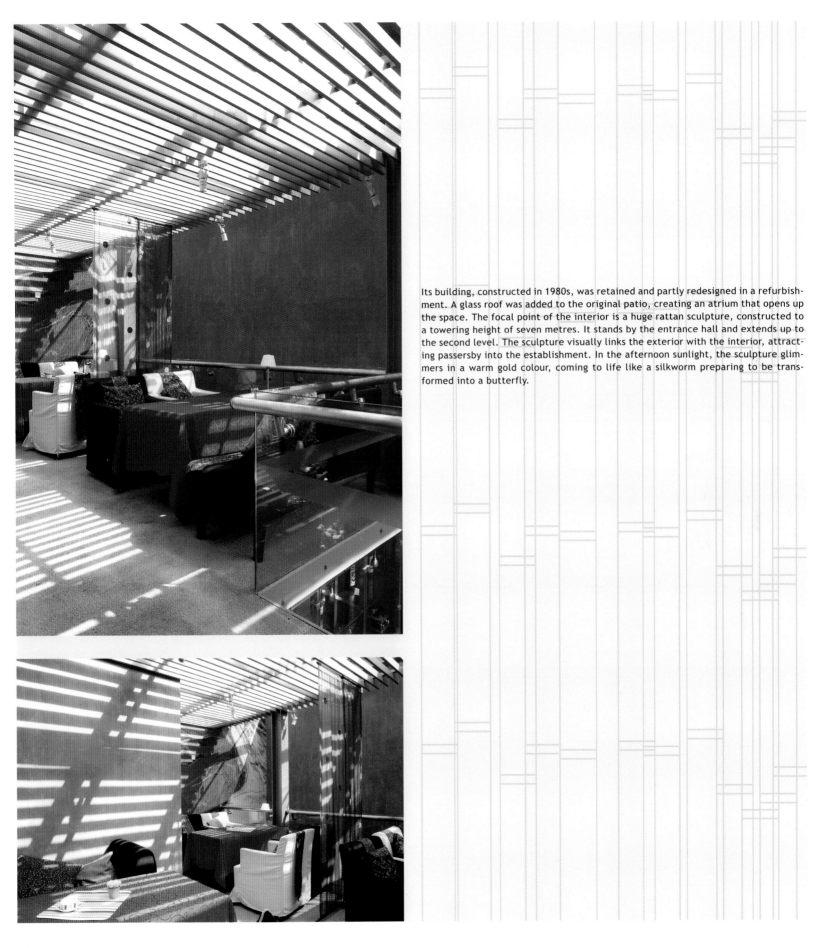

Its building, constructed in 1980s, was retained and partly redesigned in a refurbishment. A glass roof was added to the original patio, creating an atrium that opens up the space. The focal point of the interior is a huge rattan sculpture, constructed to a towering height of seven metres. It stands by the entrance hall and extends up to the second level. The sculpture visually links the exterior with the interior, attracting passersby into the establishment. In the afternoon sunlight, the sculpture glimmers in a warm gold colour, coming to life like a silkworm preparing to be transformed into a butterfly.

(this page) A display shelf adds visual interest to the interior

(opposite page: top left) Colourful abstract artwork line the walls of *Glimmering Silkworm*

(opposite page: bottom left) Seating sections are separated by delicate sheers

(opposite page: right) Bright throw cushions play off the fiery abstract artworks

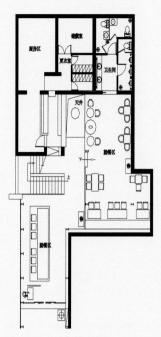

First storey floor plan

Second storey floor plan

(opposite page) The interior dining area of the first floor

(this page: top) The interior dining area of the first floor

(this page: bottom) In converting the original patio, part of the space was retained to accomodate the double volume space where the hand-woven ratten sculpture is placed

(this page) A glimpse of the VIP room

(opposite page) A huge three-dimensional artwork comprising of coloured crystal boxes at the end of main dining hall

dong lai shun
restaurant

A resident of Beijing for more than 100 years, *Dong Lai Shun* dressed itself in a clean and decent interior in a move to introduce its fantastic long-established Chinese cuisine on its new venture to Hong Kong. Located at the basement of Royal Garden Hotel, a presentation of Chinese elegance with human warmth is captured for an atypical Chinese dining experience.

The overall setting of *Dong Lai Shun* in Hong Kong is an assimilation of an old Chinese upper class residence – unobtrusive as compared to a royal palace, but extremely lavish and comfortable. Various subtle Chinese touches are found – huge lanterns with Chinese motifs, patterned private room doors and walls, as well as a combination of dark woods, golden and red shades and textures. Together, they deliver an interior with a classy Chinese ambience.

photography Ulso Tsang **designer** Steve Leung **design firm** Steve Leung Designers Limited **location** Royal Garden Hotel, Hong Kong

(this page) Entrance from the hotel's shopping arcade

(opposite page: top) One of the VIP rooms

(opposite page: bottom) Intricate ornamentation envelopes the VIP room

The restaurant has two major entrances: one from the main hotel shopping arcade, and another from a staircase directing customers from Mody Street, amid the high traffic in Tsim Sha Tsui. At this street entrance, a spectacular showcase of bluish crystal beads surrounding a medallion is placed to capture attention. Descending the staircase, another huge art-piece greets guests, preparing them for the fabulous dinner to come.

Designed for the restaurant's different entrances, two distinct focal points were set within its rectangular layout. At the end of the long dining hall where attention would fall from the direction of the staircase, hangs a huge 3-dimentional artwork. It comprises of coloured crystal boxes that reflect different colours when viewed from different angles. Upon closer inspection, traditional Chinese patterns can be found tattooed on each box, revealing a meticulous oriental style. The other focal point, when looking from the long unclosed side, would certainly be the feature wall beside the big private room where a dragon robe is hanged. Together with the high ceiling and stream of huge lanterns, the feeling of being in a Chinese theatre is central to the concept in this private room.

Since the restaurant is well-known for its sliced mutton hot pot, the designer's challenge was to present this great traditional Chinese taste in a contemporary way. The induction heating system is concealed under each table, ensuring that convenience and functionality are met while the appearance of tidiness is maintained. Warm interior lighting is concentrated at the middle of tables to maximise appreciation of food.

(this page: left) One of the bigger VIP rooms where a dragon robe serves as the backdrop

(this page: right) A closer view of the Chinese motifs that fill the restaurant and VIP rooms

(opposite page) A view of several un-partitioned VIP rooms

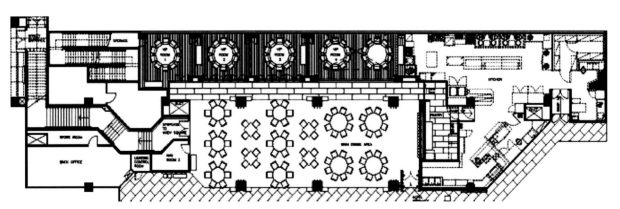

Floor plan

(opposite page) The restaurant's main dining area

(this page) One of the many fabulous Chinese artworks within the restaurant

crystal jade kitchen

Tucked away in what was previously a quiet corner of Singapore's Junction 8 Shopping Centre, *Crystal Jade Kitchen* has now transformed the sleepy shopping centre basement into a bustling scene of hungry diners.

The famous restaurant whose name is synonymous with good food, has carved out a big portion of the F&B market for themselves. The opening of the new outlet in Junction 8 Shopping Centre was part of their massive expansion across Singapore.

Standing outside the eatery, patrons are greeted by a discreet entrance with a hostess's podium and a frosted glass panel. As smells emanate from within, guests can catch glimpses of the warm and inviting interior as busy wait staff hustle about to serve hungry patrons.

The restaurant is designed in three main sections, with a central corridor serving as the main circulation medium. The main seating section lies at the end of the tiny outlet while two quiet sections - one offering booth seats and the other larger table settings - take up a side of the restaurant respectively. The main section is designed with a curved wall, bestowing an interesting tunnel effect to the section. The sweeping gesture brings a sense of movement and rhythm to the design, significantly upping its visual impact.

photography Kelley Cheng **designer** Fukumoto San **design firm** Chanto Design Pte Ltd **location** Junction 8 Shopping Centre, Singapore

(this page: left) A red wall punctuated with white columns acts as the focal point in one of the restaurant's side sections

(this page: top right) A quiet booth within the restaurant

(this page: bottom right) The clean and simple lines of the restaurant's interior elements flow through to its furniture and fittings

(opposite page) Timber slat partitions separating booth seats give the interior a sense of geometry and balance

Crystal Jade Kitchen's interior is dominated by warm colours, rich woods and subdued lighting - red, green and brown makes up the main palette, creating a cosy and conducive environment for a sumptuous meal. As light falls on timber slat partitions segmenting each section, they cast enigmatic shadows, adding to the visual appeal of the place.

In line with the Crystal Jade Group of Restaurants' new image, *Crystal Jade Kitchen* has a calm and composed ambience, fused Chinese and modern elements that give the restaurant a stylish, modern, yet distinctly Oriental atmosphere.

(this page: left) Materials within the restaurant, chosen for their clean and understated qualities

(this page: top right) Simple but aesthetically pleasing partitions segment the sections within the restaurant

(this page: bottom right) View of a side section of the restaurant, with the frosted glass facade as the foreground

(opposite page) View of the sweeping curved wall in the main dining section

(this page) A private function room designed with a touch of traditional Hangzhou charm

(opposite page) The gallery dining area has views overlooking the void above the main dining space. Across, the window treatments of the private rooms form an internal facade within the restaurant

Yi jia Xian

Upon entering the symmetrical, neo-classical facade of *Yi Jia Xian*, the simple layout and strong contrasting colours set the mood of the place. The simplicity extends behind the door into the over-two-storeys-high main hall. Engraved lattice work serves as the backdrop of the reception, running from the ground up to the ceiling. With natural light filtering through the windows, it provides a relaxed atmosphere that resembles alfresco dining on an outdoor patio.

photography Wen Zongbo **designer** Bing Zhu **design firm** Talent Architecture **location** Tian Mu Shan Road, Hangzhou

Standing in the center of the hall and looking up, one is overwhelmed by the visual impact of a tensioned membrane structure hanging from the ceiling and large, unique overhead light fixtures. Long, curved swan-neck floor lamps are used to offer direct lighting onto the tables, adding to the eccentricity and delicacy to the interior. The unconventional and irregular layout of dining tables and chairs in the hall makes full use of the space, creating order through randomness.

On the second floor, at the north part of the establishment are tables for two, where diners can overlook the whole restaurant while enjoying their food. On the west, a finely-engraved traditional stone gate and darkened doors with antique brass knockers echo the classical elements of the facade. In the private function rooms, traditional windows with coloured glass panes and background walls address a harmonious blending of old and new elements.

Simple lines, strong colours, carefully positioned lighting and elegant ornaments all blend together with strong classic flavours to form the interesting and highly dramatic interior of *Yi Jia Xian*.

(opposite page) A colourful wall painting engages as the focal point on the southern end of the restaurant

(this page: top left) A section of the main dining area, raised and segmented off on an illuminated platform

(this page: right) Through the restaurant's internal facade, guests are greeted by another dining room

(this page: bottom left) View of the main dining area, showing its double-height volume

(this page) One of restaurant's private dining rooms, flaunting a harmonious blend of old and new elements

(opposite page: top) The private room, designed in a traditional Hangzhou architectural flavour with a life-size artifact as the focal point

(opposite page: bottom) Timber lattice screen doors offer partial views into a private dining room

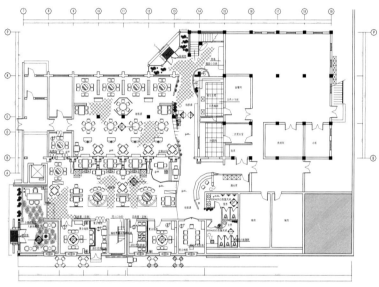

Floor plan

(this page) Booth seating in the central dining area with white-crackled paint

(opposite page) The waterfront dining room, offering unadulterated views of Victoria harbour. The green private dining room sits adjacent to the full-height windows

shanghai mian

Given the challenging task of uniting several retail units in a shopping mall to form the restaurant, the designer's concept was to fragment the space into sections.

The section immediately visible from the shopping mall is a dining area flanked by a noodle bar. Together, they form the entrance into the restaurant. A signbox with the name of the restaurant is located at the end of the corridor, beckoning diners in. The dining area is a semi-public area lined with thin white columns while a continuous flow of distinctive birdcage lamps fill the ceiling, hinting at the extensive length of the establishment.

photography Graham Uden **designer** Hernan Zanghellini **design firm** Zanghellini Holt Architects **location** World Trade Center, Causeway Bay, Hong Kong

(this page) A corner of the bar/dining area

(opposite page: top) Looking into private dining room, styled with western architraves

(opposite page: bottom) Bar dining area with the 'light columns' decorated with enlarged traditional Chinese motifs

Upon reaching the second section, different seating configurations come into view as large columns acting as lamps decorated with enlarged Chinese motifs punctuate the space. The different seating arrangements in this bar/dining area open up a variety of individual spaces to guests and adds to the experience of the restaurant. A round table with an over-sized "wok" hung upside down with two female portrait paintings set the tone for this corner.

Progressing through, one finally reaches the main central dining area, which expands into an open space that boasts magnificent views of the harbour. Aided further by its raised floor height, the central dining area is the perfect place to get unobstructed views of the harbour while enjoying a cosy afternoon lunch. This area is further divided in into zones by the raising of different floor heights. The brightness of the space was also enhanced from the previous more subdued and enclosed environment by using white-crackle paint over a base colour of red. Along the left side, a row of booth seats hugs the wall.

Moving into the back section of the restaurant, one comes upon a full-height window offering more views of the splendid Victoria harbour. Here, the view is the focal point in the interior. And on its side, a wall filled with colourful Chinese prints frames the view while a private dining room, painted in luxurious shades of green, can be found at the opposite corner.

Shanghai Mian's ingenious design serves up more than just aesthetic value – the various sections in the restaurant can be closed off for different activities throughout the day. Its theme of using different prime colours, coupled with the breaking down of sections into sub-zones with a wide variety of seating arrangements, balustrades, low partitions and transgressions of lighting has successfully created individual unique spaces within this distinctive establishment.

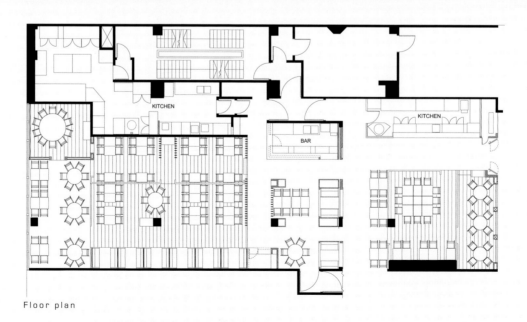

Floor plan

(opposite page) A section in the central dining area divided with low partitions and balustrades

(this page: top left) The green private dining room with an enormous overhanging "wok" lamp

(this page: top right) The restaurant's shopping mall dining area

(this page: bottom left) The entrance and main access corridor leading into the restaurant

(this page: bottom right) The bright and cheery waterfront dining room

heaven and earth

Descending a flight of stairs from the hustle and bustle of the main commercial district of central in Hong Kong, guests are greeted by a glass display wall with traditional Chinese porcelain wine vases and theatrical masks. Moving down the stairs, the mood drastically changes with subdued atmosphere of gentle lighting.

Two separate entrances denote the distinct areas of the bar and the restaurant that spawned the name *Heaven and Earth*, implying the two main elements of the establishment.

photography Graham Uden **designer** Hernan Zanghellini **design firm** Zanghellini Holt Architects **location** D'Aguilar Street, Central, Hong Kong

(this page) The rotating booths in the main dining area

(opposite page: top left) Guests are greeted by Chinese theatrical masks as they descend a flight of stairs into Heaven and Earth

(opposite page: right) View towards the rotating booth in the main dining area

(opposite page: middle left) The curved bar counter

(opposite page: bottom left) The open layout of the main dining area

Taking the entrance on the right, it leads into the bar area. An oval shaped bar counter sits in the middle of the room. In one corner, a sweeping curved screen provides bench seating with an antique wooden plate crafted in Chinese characters. Translated, the words read "A Place of Celebration". Along the far end of the wall, more discreet seating can be found. While its main function is revelry and decadence at night, the entire bar area also serves lunch during the day.

Conversely, the entrance on the left leads guests into the main dining area. While the bar and restaurant are physically divided by thin columns, visually it can be perceived as one complete space. The existing lift shift was cleverly converted into three private dining booths, decorated in green, yellow and red. These prime Chinese colours are seen repeated in other decorative elements within *Heaven and Earth*. Hanging from the ceiling in front of the booths are three lights surrounded with spiral incenses normally found in Chinese temples, casting unique decorative accent lighting to the round tables. Seating was arranged to give ample space between each table, giving guests just the right amount of privacy, and plenty of space for circulation.

Further inside the main dining area, a focal point is set by a curved booth that can actually be rotated and thus transformed into a semi-enclosed space for intimate conversations.

Viewed as a whole, *Heaven and Earth* is a cleverly designed establishment that blends its two entities, as one complete package.

(this page) The bar area with bench seating, enhanced by an antique carved wood sign engraved with the gold Chinese characters, "A Place of Celebration"

(opposite page: left) The green dining booth

(opposite page: right) Main dining area with bench seats

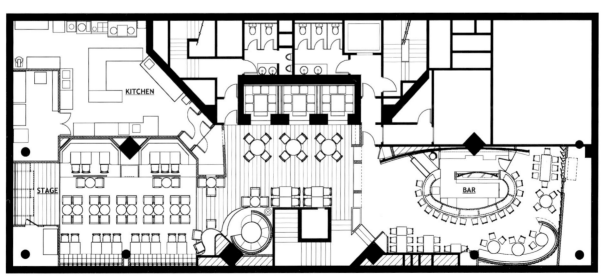

Floor plan

(this page) A dining section beside the main hall

(opposite page) The dramatic dining hall and its long feature table

crystal jade
restaurant

The design concept was to create a casual and modern Chinese restaurant with a unique identity to establish *Crystal Jade Restaurant* as an outstanding dining place in Shanghai. The owner also requested for the restaurant's design to be modern and stylish.

Upon arriving at the entrance area via the escalator, one is confronted by two curved walls, one solid and the other transparent. Using old Chinese bricks and red glazing columns, the walls give patrons a glimpse of the restaurant's interior. At the intersection of these two interwoven planes lie patterned floor tiles that lure the diners into the restaurant.

photography Liu Sheng Hui   **designer** Yasuhiro Koichi   **design firm** Design Studio SPIN   **location** Xintiandi, Shanghai

Once inside, a long neutral corridor – flanked by white walls and glass showcases looking into the kitchen and wine cellars – leads guests into the restaurant and opens up into a spacious dining hall. Here, a long dining table with an illuminated frosted glass table top dominates the space and transforms into its focal point. A mirror suspended over the table further enhances the space, visually extending its volume and doubling the impact. Bench seats arranged on the left side are subdivided by a plane of red columns with semi-private rooms placed beyond. This segmentation succeeds in creating individual spaces within the restaurant, giving character to each interior zone. The designer integrated the restaurant's existing columns and walls into its new design; red glazed columns and old Chinese bricks expressing the interaction between old and new.

The designer's aim was to create a modern space composed with a calm, oriental ambience infused with Chinese elements. The private rooms, treated with subdued colour schemes, provide an otherwise warm and cosy balance to the striking restaurant.

(opposite page: top) Dining in the main hall

(opposite page: bottom) A smaller section within the dining hall

(this page: top) The entrance corridor, leading to the main hall

(this page: bottom) An alternate view of the hall dining area

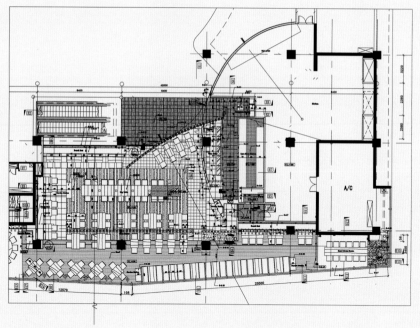

Floor plan

(opposite page) The restaurant's entrance hints at the drama to come

(this page: top) One of the semi-private rooms

(this page: bottom) One of the bigger semi-private rooms with a long dining table (this page) In the evening, the colourful oriental interior is clearly revealed and cast onto the street level facade. Its presence draws a sharp contrast to the bland commercial buildings in the surrounding

(opposite page) This space, deliberately left empty, functions as the central hallway where people can flow into surrounding secondary spaces

Marunouchi cafe

The area of Marunouchi has long been established as a business centre since the 1970's. Widely regarded and maintained as the cosmopolitan district in Tokyo, Japan, showrooms, sales offices and banking facilities occupy the ground floors of the buildings.

The arrival of *Marunouchi Cafe* was like a breath of fresh air to this area. This was part of the developer's concept to re-position the area with fashion and lifestyle stores such as Calvin Klein, Burberry, Comme de Garcons, Baccarat and the like, transforming the street level into an upmarket retail district. The developer, Mitsubishi Estate Ltd, owns a total of thirty out of the fifty buildings in the Marunouchi area.

photography Alan Chan **designer** Wong Kin Ho and Alan Chan **design firm** Workshop and Alan Chan Design Company
architect MEC Design International Corporation, **location** Fuji Building, Chiyoda-ku, Tokyo, Japan

130

(opposite page) The symmetrical setting frames the entrance to *Marunouchi Cafe*, further emphasised by highlights of red in the lanterns and columns. Its warm and cosy ambience is visible from the outside

(this page: top left) A mundane area has been successfully transformed into an interesting place: the cafe's vending machines are blended into antique furniture with oriental characteristics while its backdrop is made up of empty tin cans. The display of the colourful toys hung from the ceiling are all made of leftover tins bought from Vietnam

(this page: top right) The customers indulge in their own leisurely activities within the cafe

(this page: bottom) A custom-made wood frame hanging above echoes the cafe's long table

(this page) With the glass doors open, the circular arch acts as a divider between the external and internal space, creating a transitional space that allows the street to become part of the cafe, and cafe part of the street (this page: top) With various art exhibitions featured regularly, the exhibition area provides a wonderful space for art appreciation. The vertical columns, originally an obstacle to the space, were wrapped with red Thai silk printed with various Asian characters as visual statements

(this page: bottom) The round tables have white marble tops with traditional Chinese wood-crafted bases. The chairs were selected from different periods of various Asian countries. The white freestanding wall with Chinese motifs further divide the space

Located within this business district, the *Marunouchi Cafe* stands out prominently. It makes an impact with a transparent facade that reveals its oriental atmosphere, creating a contrast to the bland office buildings in the area. Since its opening, it has become an oasis within a business centre, inviting people to wander into the space in search for a quiet and relaxing moment. The place comprises of a gallery, IT space, promotion area, vending machine room and a relaxing space for patrons.

While the decor is predominantly Asian, spiced with contemporary paintings and posters, it changes periodically as the cafe also acts as an exhibition space for artists. The idea is to create an Asian atmosphere that differentiates itself from the western and high-tech office buildings. However, the Cafe blends its own modern technological facilities with antique furniture, selected and imported from Mainland China and South East Asian countries such as Singapore and Indonesia. Together, they give *Marunouchi Cafe* a wonderful blend of beauty, tradition and tranquility that bring humanity back to the everyday life buried under the apathy of IT.

134

peerless teahouse

As an ancient capital with a long history, Hangzhou is now losing more and more of its typical old buildings due to the city's dynamic development in recent years. The concern of this transformation has led to the basis of the design of *Peerless Teahouse*.

Located at the beautiful West Lake and occupying an approximate area of 2,500 square metres, *Peerless Teahouse* was originally a freestanding pseudo-classic style building built in 1992. Its unique location and architectural design induced its designer to reposition it as a modern building with local cultural characteristics, achieved by employing both traditional clay bricks and modern steel structures as the dominant elements that are arranged orderly throughout the whole space.

photography Courtesy of Talent Architecture   **designer** Zheng Yao   **design firm** Talent Architecture   **location** Bao Shu Road, Hangzhou

136

(this page: left) A mix of old and new materials create a
contemporary atmosphere

(this page: right) The traditional lotus pond is reinterpreted, using
a contemporary approach

(opposite page) The use of Chinese wood screens brings transparency
to the interior while allowing views of the exterior

The interior of *Peerless Teahouse* is user-oriented with clay bricks and glass used as partition materials. On the exterior, the modern steel structure is juxtaposed with traditional elements like white walls, black tiles, clay bricks and a moon gate, displaying an alternative expression of classic architecture. A large turtle-like bronze sculpture and dark coloured curved steel eaves also add a feeling of raw simplicity to the exterior.

The teahouse is divided into three levels: the first level, part of which is the entrance hall, offers loose seating for consumers. A traditional Chinese kiosk equipped with Ming-styled backrests is introduced as the visual focus, forming a strong contrast with the modern mural in the entrance lift hall. On the second floor, private rooms with natural clay bricks and sandblasted glass partitions create an aura of simplicity, elegance and modernity. The third floor presents a vivacious spatial experience, enriched by rise and falls in the floor. Clay-brick partitions of various forms, put together with the dark blue interior fabrics, provide privacy without breaking the continuity of space. In the day when sunlight streams into the building, custom-made lattices on the door cast patterned shadows on the floor, bestowing an added layer of visual splendor to the interior.

(opposite page: top left) The *Peerless Teahouse*'s quiet and cosy ambience

(opposite page: top right) Traditional building materials are partnered perfectly with rustic modern furnishings

(opposite page: bottom left) Custom-made lattices cast patterned shadows on the floor during the day, bestowing an added layer of visual splendor to the interior

(this page) On the third level, segmentation of zones benefit from the introduction of various floor levels

(opposite page) A secluded dining area on the third level

(this page: top left) View of the teahouse's skylight

(this page: top right) Stairs with illuminated risers decorated with intricate wood lattices

(this page: bottom left) A passageway on the second level

(this page) The restaurant's facade and main entrance

(opposite page) The elongated bar table is one of the features of the dining space; to the right, glazed partitions separate the main dining space from the private rooms, providing both privacy and transparency

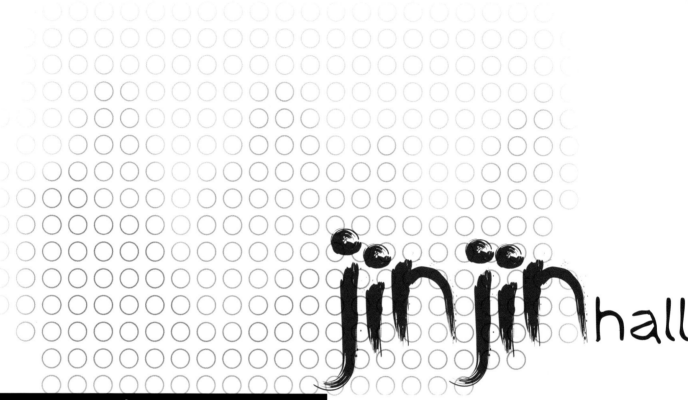

jin jin hall

Located in the Suzhou Industrial Park, *Jin Jin Hall* is a seafood hotpot restaurant whose design concept was to break away from the conventional Chinese restaurant but retain a simple and pure environment for guests.

By dividing the usually long and narrow site into zones, a row of glowing transparent posts are employed as the border between the hall and private rooms to create a sense of depth. Gray cement flooring dominates the entire space as the main element while glass partitions decorated with coloured films are used as translucent screens. In the middle of the dining hall, long high-tables set another visual focal point echoed with long cylindrical lighting above. The extractor hoods over the window-side tables have glass covers which are filled by specimens of sea animals.

photography Wen Zongbo **designer** Bing Zhu **design firm** Talent Architecture **location** Suzhou Industrial Park, Suzhou

(opposite page) The bright red patterned glass creates a dramatic contrast against the restaurant's dark and serene environment

(this page: left)The row of glass partitions separating the private rooms from the main dining area

(this page: top right) Subdued colours are used throughout the dining area

(this page: bottom right) The restaurant's black palette extends up to the ceiling, decreasing the sense of compression from the low ceiling

(this page) Subdued colours are combining wood panels, black floor tiles and grey curtains

(opposite page) Above the tables, extractor fans are hidden in decorative display boxes

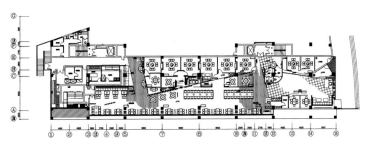

Floor plan

The colour scheme for the restaurant is predominantly black and orange. Black extends up to the ceiling, decreasing the sense of compression from the low ceiling, while the eye-catching orange columns act as dividers of the internal space.

Jin Jin Hall's palette signals a breakaway from the traditional Chinese colour scheme of red and brown, while maintaining a feeling of warmth throughout the restaurant. Here, orange is a modern representation of red, while black gives a new twist to the colour brown. Similarly, its grey cement flooring also denotes a modern interpretation of traditional stone flooring.

With an inventive array of modern materials and contemporary colours, *Jin Jin Hall* gives a new life to the traditional hotpot cuisine.

(this page) The entrance to the teahouse bears a distinctly Oriental style

(opposite page) The double volume atrium makes for a dramatic entrance. Water and natural garden elements abound in the interior

Suzhou Cha ren cottage

Located adjacent to Baihuazhou inside the old city wall of the Xu Gate, Suzhou, the teahouse is a new building with an area of about 1,000 square metres, surrounded by brick walls and greenery creating a natural setting for tea lovers.

Jiangnan gardens bear a tradition of stressing on context and artistic conception. Plants with over hundred species, tablets and stones of various forms and scenic views in the surrounding add to the appreciation of enjoying a cup of tea.

It is the intention of the designer to create an interior with a simple and minimal approach which emulates the spirit of simplicity seen in traditional Jiangnan gardens. Gray blue granite panels hung throughout the interior as partitions, together with the use of transparent glass, form enclosed private spaces and yet visual connections are allowed between these individual spaces.

photography Liu Shenghui   **designer** Yi Wen Chen   **design firm** Talent Architecture   **location** Bai Hua Zhou Road, Suzhou

(opposite page: top left) One of the private spaces within the teahouse

(opposite page: top right) Modern grey-blue granite walls, traditional dark wood Chinese furniture and artworks make for a poetic sight

(opposite page: bottom left) The lines of the granite walls, viewed against the strong lines of the furniture, evoke a strong sense of symmetry and order

(opposite page: bottom right) The retail section of the teahouse is a picture of calm

(this page) A quiet corner in the teahouse, composed with a sensitive play of material, texture and colour

(opposite page) Bright spots of colour give a visual kick to the otherwise quiet interior

(this page: top left) A moongate gives context to the teahouse within its traditional surroundings

(this page: top right) A table overlooks the serene grounds of Jiangnan gardens as sunlight bathes the teahouse in a soft, dreamy light

(this page: bottom left) The remarkable beauty of stone, seen here against the simple lines of the teahouse's sculpted Chinese furniture; the composition – of raw stone against refined furniture – a metaphor in itself

(this page) The restaurant facade

(opposite page) A view of the main dining area, looking towards the entrance

cheena restaurant

The setting of *Cheena* has the kind of sophisticated elegance that combines Oriental influence with modernism, filled with affluence and grace. Designed with fine furnishings and rich materials, it has a gentle and lavish splendour with touches of Chinese beauty.

A Chinese style rectangular wood box graces the restaurant's entrances while a glowing 'lightbox' column and curved transparent glass accentuates *Cheena's* entrance, portraying the restaurant's strong Oriental influence at first glance. Behind lies a semi-circular private area, delicately shaped by the curved transparent wall at the entrance and complemented by a simple railing and flexible satin curtains.

Entering the restaurant, one is greeted by a vision of class. Silver wallpapered backdrops, plush upholstery and opulent lights seduce patrons, drawing them into this world of absolute elegance. The restaurant is laid out in two basic areas – the main dining hall and the private area. The main dining hall offers patrons several seating options of conventional table or bench seating. The bench areas, flushed to the side of the restaurant, features a high back rest upholstered in luxurious fabrics.

Within the main dining hall, *Cheena's* feature wall decorated with illuminated niches and artifacts is distinctive, yielding the key for Chinese cultural stylishness. Meanwhile in the main dining area, hanging lamps light up the beauty of *Cheena's* culinary offerings. Tall windows bring in sunlight through modern yet elegant wood frames of traditional Chinese details. Interior mirror placements are constructive – carefully positioned to visually extend the volume of the restaurant.

The warm lighting and earthy tones inspire patrons to revive their spirituality through a peaceful and relaxing meal in the beautiful environment of *Cheena* restaurant.

photography Ulso Tsang   **designer** Steve Leung   **design firm** Steve Leung Designers Limited   **location** Rosedale Hotel, Hong Kong

(this page: top left) Tall windows bring sunlight into the interior

(this page: top right) A view of the restaurant's interior, looking towards the entrance

(this page: bottom) A view of the main dining area's bench seating

(opposite page: top) The private room, separated by soft satin curtains

(opposite page: bottom left) The private dining area is decorated with special Chinese artifacts and rectangular pendant lamps

(opposite page: bottom right) The restaurant's entrance

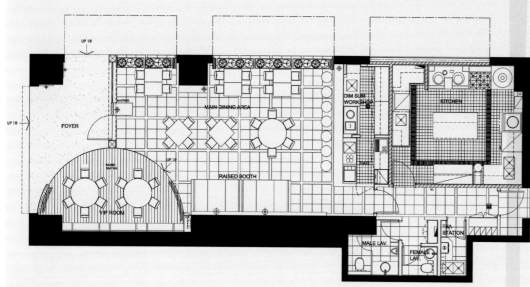

Floor plan

(this page) The restaurant's show kitchen enhances the feeling of spaciousness

(opposite page) A view of the restaurant from the private dining area

(this page) Overlooking the coffee shop from the staircase landing

(opposite page) The coffee shop's double volume height enriches the feeling of openness without stripping its warm and cosy ambience

haikou new world garden resort clubhouse

160

Situated in Haikou City of Hainan Island, the southeast province of China, the Haikou New World Garden Resort is only twenty minutes from the airport highway exit. The clubhouse is designed to screen off the main road from the resort property in order to preserve privacy and blend in with the magnificent natural environment. The secluded landscaped garden surrounding the clubhouse provides a sense of tropical living, creating a sense of cosiness and intimacy.

The architecture of the building pays tribute to the local Haikou materials, using coconut palms, terracotta-hued tiles, flamed granite and crushed volcanic rock that together, create a sense of place. Although the estate is screened by lush greenery, the designers raised the clubhouse to give it a greater sense of privacy.

Upon arrival, guests are greeted by an open-air entrance foyer overlooking the entire coffee shop, and a reflecting pool that wraps itself around the clubhouse's exterior. Behind a rustic stonewall, a discreet stairway leads down to the coffee shop below where staircases on the both sides lead directly into activity rooms by way of a connecting bridge-like corridor. Towering over the lower floors of the clubhouse, the corridor brings an arresting double volume experience to the spaces below.

The clubhouse facilities include reading rooms, a bar lounge, a coffee shop, a banquet room, two VIP rooms, two multi-function rooms, a table tennis room, activity rooms for elderly and children, wine cellars, cigar rooms, exercise rooms, a health center and outdoor pool facilities.

Tied together by a rustic yet modern central design theme, tranquil surroundings, striking architecture and comfortable furnishings, the *Haikou New World Garden Resort Clubhouse* makes for an excellent getaway.

photography Thomas Chan   **designer** Thomas Chan   **design firm** Thomas Chan Designs Limited   **location** Xinfou Island, Haikou, China

(opposite page) Tall windows with full-height timber panelling that can be opened in summer for natural ventilation bring steady streams of sunlight in while presenting tranquil views of the garden beyond

(this page: top left) A carved stonewall panel echoes floor patterns in the entrance foyer

(this page: right) A stonewall fountain and reflecting pool provides soothing sounds of flowing water to the coffee shop

(this page: bottom left) The sloped ceiling in wood cladding allows good ventilation, airflow and light penetration

(opposite page) One of the clubhouse's washrooms, designed in strong forms and natural materials

(this page: left) View from the corridor, overlooking the coffee shop with a glimpse of the entrance foyer on the left

(this page: right) The clubhouse's bar lounge

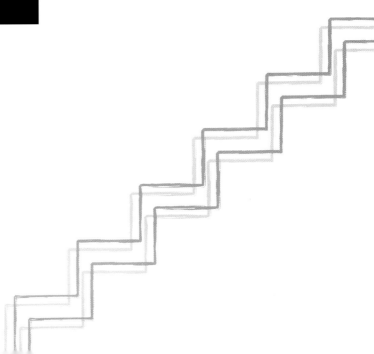

(this page) The traditional dark wood elements of the entrance echoes the dark wood floors and antique furniture of the interior

(opposite page) Exterior of the 1928's building where *Ye Shanghai* is located

ye shanghai

Ye Shanghai **is located** in a historic "Shikumen" stone gate house in Xintiandi. The former historic French Concession, Xintiandi is noted for its many historic buildings which have been carefully restored to their original splendor.

The challenge posed to internationally-renowned designer, Tony Chi, was how to balance the traditional elements of the 1928's building with a new modern feel. He started with the set of inherited traditional design vocabulary, and added a second vocabulary of modern components, resulting in a contemporary Chinese style that is anything but predictable and yet manages to capture a sense of the times past.

photography Chester Ong **designer** Tony Chi **design firm** Elite Concept **location** Xintiandi, Shanghai

Traditional features like dark wood floors, beams, and the slate roof were maintained. However, the internal spatial organisation gave way to a more open room, replacing the traditional layout with several small chambers. A gallery serving as an entryway was also incorporated into the restaurant's design. And perched above the main dining room is a balcony dining area – an untraditional touch integrated beautifully with *Ye Shanghai's* design. Guests sit in booths that reinterpret old Asian teahouse booths, but rather than having people face each other like they did in the old days, the new U-shaped booths bring people side-by-side. This is used to soften the formality of the dining environment. Formality, when required, is provided by the main dining room on the upper level, which is sheltered by the building's roof.

And in a style that has since become its signature; each of *Ye Shanghai's* four private rooms was designed with a different look. The idea is inspired by the old Chinese nobleman's house, which would have a parlor, a painting room, and various chambers for different purposes. The elegant rooms feature original art pieces and sculpture of different styles, promising guests a refreshing and fascinating experience each time around.

(opposite page) A private dining room on the ground level, framed by full-height windows that reveal contemporary paintings beyond

(this page: left) The main entrance of *Ye Shanghai*, integrated as part of the building's exterior

(this page: top right) U-shaped booths are reminiscent of the old Chinese teahouse booths

(this page: bottom) A skylight illuminates the ground floor dining area while U-shaped booths are situated off the main space

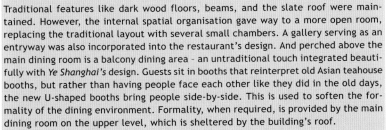

(this page: left) One of the contemporary paintings within the restaurant

(this page: top right) An antique bronze artifact placed near the upper stairs landing

(this page: bottom right) An alcove serves as a waiting area for guests

(opposite page) The formal dining area is located on the upper level, enclosed by the traditional slate roof and wooden frame structure

(this page) The Spring Blossom suite, decked out in a western decor with minimal Chinese artworks, lamps and artifacts

(opposite page) Deep seats with a black lacquer screen backdrop looking into the adjacent courtyard

Michel
house

In Dongguan, a cosmopolitan city where numerous international firms have set up operations, San Interiors was commissioned to design a 15,000 square metres corporate complex. The complex comprises of offices, recreational facilities, guest rooms and dormitories for the staff, giving designers the freedom to explore several styles under one expansive roof.

The design took the direction of incorporating Western aesthetic into Chinese style. The space is a fusion of Oriental and Western designs with abstract decorations and geometric furniture, used to create a refreshing Oriental look. The richness of the interior, firmly rooted with a traditional Chinese appearance, is gradually increased from the entrance level to the upper levels.

The lower floors devoted to the reception and administration areas are the least ornamented. Entering the building via a foyer that features a pure white wall cast with the company logo, one is also greeted by a bold red curved staircase with various elements painted in bold red.

The four upper floors are occupied by dormitories for workers, directors, clerical and executive staff, as well as recreational facilities like a library, gym, karaoke room, restaurant and teahouse. One of the most impressive areas, however, is the fifth floor with its six executive guest rooms that are individually named and themed.

photography courtesy of San Interiors   **chief designer** San Leung   **location** Dongguan, China

(this page) Two chairs placed in the center of the room, traditionally reserved for the masters of the house, emphasises the strong geometry of oriental design

(this page: left) A staircase leading up to the reception area

(this page: top right) The Great Shanghai suite provides a lavish atmosphere with red walls and Chinese artwork

(this page: bottom right) Details of the staircase railing, ornamented with oversized but simplified ancient Chinese coins

(opposite page) The conference room, designed with strong, simple lines and a feature drop-ceiling wood frame

(this page: top) Lanterns adorned with the Chinese characters that denote the word "tea"

(this page: bottom) A "wheel of mantra" originating from a Buddhist temple in Tibet marks the entrance to the teahouse

(this page: left) Screen doors with intricate detailling separate the seating area from the courtyard

(opposite page) The Pearl River suite is bathed in tranquility with simple lines, muted colours, and visually anchored with a large ornamented Chinese four-poster bed

(this page: top) The dining hall for the staff, with bar counter seats on one side

(this page: bottom) The director's room, filled with ancient geometric patterns and sombre, classic colours

The character of these rooms follows two basic themes: exquisite tranquility or lavish extravagance. As their names suggest, the Glorious Moon, Pearl River and Blue Moon Suites follow the former course: there are elements such as glazed tiles, elm panels and ivory and beige colours imparting a touch of Lingnan style to their occupants. Conversely, the Peach Blossom, Great Shanghai and Spring Blossom Suites take the latter theme of extravagance with vibrant red walls and lavish furnishings.

Above the executive floor is the director's exclusive apartment, decorated with fine Qing-style furniture along with some Western artifacts and abstract paintings. The components include a teahouse, a wine den and rooms for both Chinese and Western dining, all fused together in perfect harmony.

(this page: left) View from the corridor looking towards the reception area. The ceiling beams, pendant lamps and wall lights further define the structure and order of the space

(this page: right) A spacious grand hall leads to the seating area for relaxation and having Chinese tea while conference rooms are located on both sides with glass enclosure

(this page) The entrance to the restaurant

(opposite page) A circular private dining room, defined by elegant beaded curtains and a raised platform

si chuan dou hua restaurant

The geometric perfection of the circle and square have for centuries been a source of insurmountable visual and ideological satisfaction. The infinite elegance of the former, and the strength and rationality of the latter, seem the ultimate polar expressions of formal perfection. The design of *Si Chuan Dou Hua Restaurant* has been driven by a quest for this same sense of exquisiteness.

The sixtieth floor of Kenzo Tange's UOB Plaza 1 building in central Singapore resonates deeply with the domain of *Si Chuan Dou Hua* - a lavish Chinese restaurant targeting a mature corporate clientele that expects nothing short of perfection. Elegance and luxury were the orders for the designers at local firm PT.ID, who were lavished with a tremendous budget for the restaurant fit-out. The exclusivity of the restaurant is, of course, augmented by its lofty locale, which affords spectacular views of the city and surrounding seascape.

photography Kelley Cheng **designer** Warren Chen, Ong Seng Chwan, Faye Ong and Evelyn Lee **design firm** PT.ID Pte Ltd **location** UOB Plaza 1, Singapore

(opposite page) Luxury that abounds in the sophisticated Chinese restaurant

(this page: left) Sheer screens act as partitions within the restaurant

(this page: right) Decorative wall features composed of round dishes set within square framework consolidate the circular theme

(this page: left) The geometric perfection of the circle and square is evident throughout the restaurant

(this page: right) Window frames of brass and walnut hark back to the configuration of old Chinese copper coins

(opposite page) Geometric light features compliment the design theme, enhancing the restaurant's luxurious interior

Hardly surprising then, is the luxury that abounds. A feeling of "modern old-fashioned" elegance pervades throughout the interior. A recurrent "circular" theme establishes a unique aesthetic structure. This begins at the reception area, immediately after one exits the lift lobby. Behind a rounded hostess podium, two curved wall panels of brass mosaic tiles are set between dark curving walls. A secondary design discourse of gaps and glimpses is also hereby established, with slivers of the impressive sixtieth-floor view beckoning from between the wall panels. This is an interior that reveals itself, and its view, slowly and teasingly – much like the way the many courses of a Chinese banquet are gradually presented and consumed.

Decorative elements consolidate the circular theme – most notably, wall features composed of round green, white and blood coloured dishes set within square framework, and window frames of brass and walnut. The latter, grandly scaled compositions of squares circumscribed with circles, make for perfect viewing portals through which to take in the spectacular view. Simultaneously, they hark back to the configuration of old Chinese copper coins, which were round with a central square hole. The pure geometry of the window frames is elsewhere abstracted – for example, in a timber and onyx wall feature (depicting the moon and clouds) set above a row of banquette seating.

Locally conceived artwork rounds off the *Si Chuan Dou Hua* experience. Singapore based artist Christine Mak was commissioned to produce a series of ten teacups hand painted with images of children at play. These have been re-worked into wall paintings and tableware, completing an exquisite journey into geometry, visibility, material and texture.

(this page) Blood-red dishes make for decorative wall features

(opposite page: top) The restaurant's grandly scaled windows – compositions of squares circumscribed with circles

(opposite page: bottom) A view of the main dining area

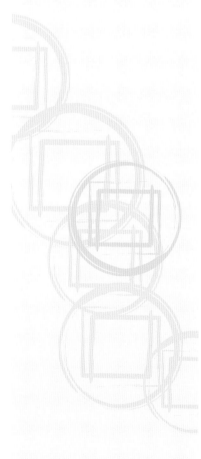

188

Floor plan

designer index

AB Concept Limited
1/F, 22 Queen's Road East Wanchai
Hong Kong China
Tel: (852) 2277 6212
Fax: (852) 2854 1038
info@abconcept.com.hk

Alan Chan Design Company
1901 Harcourt House
36 Gloucester Road Wanchai
Hong Kong China
Tel: (852) 2527 8228
Fax: (852) 2865 6170
acdesign@alanchandesign.com

Chanto Design Pte Limited
545 Orchard Road #11-01
Far East Shopping Centre
Singapore 238882
Tel: (65) 6235 0206
Fax: (65) 6235 0663
chanto@singnet.com.sg

CL3
1/F St. John's Building
33 Garden Road Central
Hong Kong China
Tel: (852) 2527 1931
Fax: (852) 2529 8392
cl3@cl3.com

Design Studio SPIN
Luceria-OB, 2-13-21 Tomigaya
Shibuya-ku, Tokyo 1510063
Japan
Tel: (81) 3 6407 2055
Fax: (81) 3 6407 2088
spin@msb.biglobe.ne.jp

Elite Concepts
G/F Hang Tak Building
1 Electric Street Wanchai
Hong Kong China
Tel: (852) 2521 0756
Fax: (852) 2596 0283
info@elite-concepts.com

EC STUDIO MANILA INC.
Unit 301 One Magnificent Mile
Condominium
39 San Miguel Avenue Ortigas Center
Pasig City Manila Philippines
Tel: (632) 633 2433
Fax: (632) 637 2040
noelb@ecstudio.com

GBRH
Hervé Bourgeois- Guillaume Richard
5 rue de Saintonge
75003 Paris France
Tel: (33) 1 42 77 53 47
Fax: (33) 1 42 77 53 69
herve@gbrh.com

IMH interiors
5 rue Las Cases
75007 Paris France
Tel : (33) 1 45 51 63 87
Fax : (33) 1 45 51 38 16
showroom@indiamahdavi.com

Joseph Sy & Associates
17/F Heng Shan Centre
145 Queen's Road East Wanchai
Hong Kong China
Tel: (852) 2866 1333
Fax: (852) 2866 1222
design@jsahk.com

MEC Design International Corporation
Cosmo Kanasugibashi Bldg. 10-11
Shiba 1-chome Minato-ku Tokyo Japan
Tel: (81) 3 6400 9000
Fax: (81) 3 6400 9071
bp@mecdesign.co.jp

Plan 3 Asia Limited
8/F Carfield Commercial Building
77 Wyndham Street Central
Hong Kong China
Tel: (852) 2525 3037
Fax: (852) 2845 2183
plan3ltd@biznetvigator.net

PT.ID Pte Ltd
10 Jiak Chuan Road
Singapore 089264
Tel: (65) 62273698
Fax: (65) 2248032
ptarchitects@pacific.net.sg

San Interiors
1727 Top Sail Plaza
11 On Sum Street Shatin
Hong Kong China
Tel: (852) 2690 3165
Fax: (852) 2690 3162
info@saninteriors.com.hk

Steve Leung Designers Limited
9/F Block C Seaview Estate
8 Watson Road North Point
Hong Kong China
Tel: (852) 2527 1600
Fax: (852) 2527 2071
sla@steveleung.com.hk

Talent Architecture
5 Hangzhou Changning Road
Hangzhou Zhejiang China
Tel: (86) 571 87922468
Fax: (86) 571 87039466
talent@hztalent.com

Thomas Chan Designs Limited
12A & 13A Hang Seng Centre
95-97 Tung Chau Street Kowloon
Hong Kong China
Tel: (852) 2308 1280
Fax: (852) 2308 1350
enquiry@thomaschan.hk

Zanghellini & Holt
2C Riviera Mansion
59-65 Paterson Street
Causeway Bay
Hong Kong China
Tel: (852) 2914 2563
Fax: (852) 2914 2675
hz@zanghellini.com

acknowledgements

We would like to thank all the architects, designers for their kind permission to publish their works; all the photographers who have generously granted us permission to use their images, and most of all, to all the establishments who have so graciously allow us to photograph their premises and to share them with readers the world over. Also, thank you to all those who have helped in one way or another in putting together this book.

Thank you all.